Easy
String Art For All Seasons

By
Darline Later Andelin

Index
from easiest to most difficult

Star	(very very easy)	Summer
Heart	(very very easy)	February
Christmas Tree	(very very easy)	December
Gift	(very very easy)	Birthdays, December
Flower	(very very easy)	May
Witch's Hat	(very very easy)	October
Sail Boat	(very easy)	Summer
Slate	(very easy)	September
Four Leaf Clover	(very easy)	March
Umbrella	(very easy)	April
Crayon	(very easy)	September
Kite	(very easy)	March
Stop Sign	(very easy)	September
Pencil	(very easy)	September
Clock	(very easy)	September
Mitten	(very easy)	January
Butterfly	(very easy)	Spring
Angel Fish	(very easy)	All year
Egg	(very easy)	April
Ice Cream in a Cone	(very easy)	Summer
Tepee	(easy)	November
Donut	(easy)	All year
Pear	(easy)	Fall
U.S. Flag	(easy)	All year
Tie	(easy)	June
Spring Flower	(easy)	May
Christmas Decoration	(easy)	December
Flowers in a Pot	(easy)	May
Balloon	(easy)	All year
Ice Cream on a Stick	(easy)	Summer
Christmas Light	(easy)	December
Football	(easy)	Fall

ISBN 1-56861-047-5

Copyright © 1996 by Darline Later Andelin. Published and printed in the United States of America by Swift Learning Resources, 88 North West State Rd., American Fork, Utah 84003. All rights reserved. Permission is given the purchaser to copy patterns for use in their own classroom or home. Copies may not be distributed to other classrooms or homes without written permission from the publisher.

JUSTIFICATION

The use of string art is not only a fun activity for children, it reinforces math concepts. String art is directly related to geometry. It can be used to demonstrate geometric concepts and vocabulary. String art helps to develop logical thinking and deductive reasoning as well as demonstrating spatial relationships. It also reinforces patterning.

Using the instructions with each pattern teaches the child the necessity of following directions in a correct sequence. When a mistake is made, the error is quite visible, so immediate feedback is provided.

This is an activity that is a real boost to a child's self-confidence. Because the patterns have a difficulty level provided, you can choose the pattern that will meet even a younger child's ability to complete a project in a reasonable amount of time. Once the string art is done, the child will have a project he/she can be proud of.

As a child develops skill in the completing of different designs, he/she begins to see ways of making up his/her own string art pictures.

MATERIALS NEEDED

- Push Pins
- #20 Tapestry Needle
- Tape
- Scissors
- Pattern
- Punch pad
- Bedspread weight crochet thread in color desired to complete work.
- Piece of poster board 7"X7" (Notes: 12 7X7 pieces can be cut form one piece of poster board. Cardboard from cereal boxes, stockings, etc. can also be used.
- Colored paper to back picture and Paper clips (opt.)

1. Cut out pattern leaving directions attached. (A) The directions can be cut off once the project is completed.

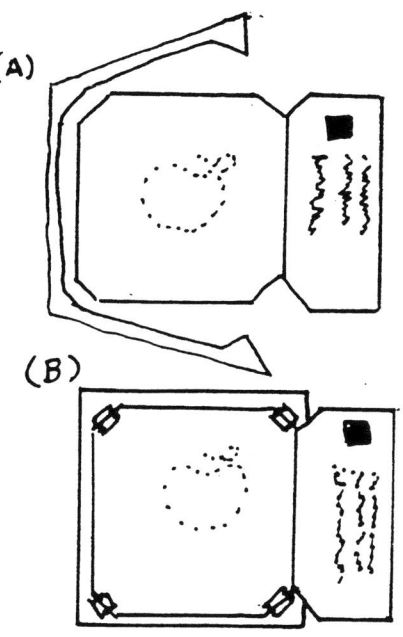

2. Tape pattern to wrong side of the cardboard. (B)

3. With push pin, poke holes through the pattern and the cardboard. Cushion the cork by uing a carpet square, the carpeted floor, or other padded surface.

4. The numbers under the down column indicate the hole where the needle passes down from the wrong side to the right side of the work. The numbers under the up column indicate the hole where the needle passes up from the right side to the wrong side of the picture. Work the stitches going down each column. The numbering is designed to give a minimum amount of long stitches on the wrong side of the picture.

5. Cut thread. Do not cut thread too long because this will cause the thread to tangle easily. About 1-1/2 yards is a good length to work with.

6. Thread needle. Commercial needle threaders can be used or you can cut one from the paper scraps of the pattern. To make a paper needle threader, cut a strip of paper 1/2" X 1". Fold the strip in half lengthwise. (Paper is now 4" X 1".) (C) Place the thread on the fold of the "Threader" and close over the thread. Push the "threader" with the thread enclosed through the eye of the needle. (D)

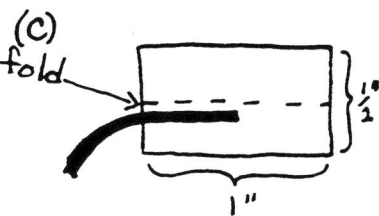

7. Position the thread so the double thread will not slip out of the needle's eye and yet allow stitches to be sewn with a single thread. Do not tie the thread to the eye as the knot will enlarge the hole of the picture while sewing. As you work the pattern the single strand of thread will be used up and you will find you reach the double thread. Slide the thread through the eye to keep a single thread and sew again. (E)

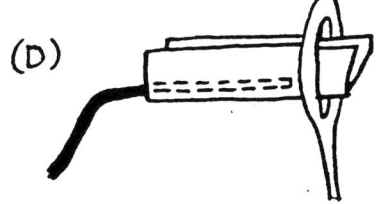

8. Tape the end of the thread close to the numbered hole to be sewn first. (F) If using other than clear tape, do not cover the numbers or the holes of the pattern.

9. When a thread is too short to work another stitch, or when changing colors, tape the thread to the wrong side of the pattern and cut off excess thread. Add a new piece of thread by repeating step 8.

10. The pattern can be left on the back when the work is completed by cutting away the directions. If you wish to remove the pattern, remove the tape from the thread ends, carefully cut or tear away the pattern from the stitches, then retape the thread ends.

11. Completed pictures can be framed, left unframed, used to make greeting cards, etc.

12. Pictures can have added color by using different colors of paper to identify parts of the picture. Paperclip all colors to be used to the cardboard before punching holes. Trim shapes using the holes as a guide. Place colors on cardboard before sewing.

13. By reducing patterns two times at a 65% reduction, pictures are small enough to put in a 3" hoop. When working pictures use embroidery thread and needle instead of crochet thread and tapestry needle. Those pictures, reduced once should also use embroidery thread and needle. Instead of using a push pin for reduced work, wrap masking tape around a straight pin to provide a handle allowing about 1/4" of the pin to show. This will make smaller holes which is necessary because of their closeness.

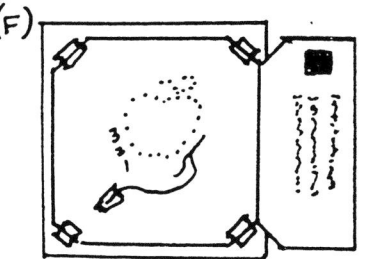

Note: These patterns can be used on fabric, but are not recommended for children. This is qu.'e complicated and requires the fabric to be stabilized with iron-on stiffening and an embroidery hoop. It is recommended that the pattern be stitched on through each dot to identify dots from the right side as the holes close up and cannot be seen to work the pattern.

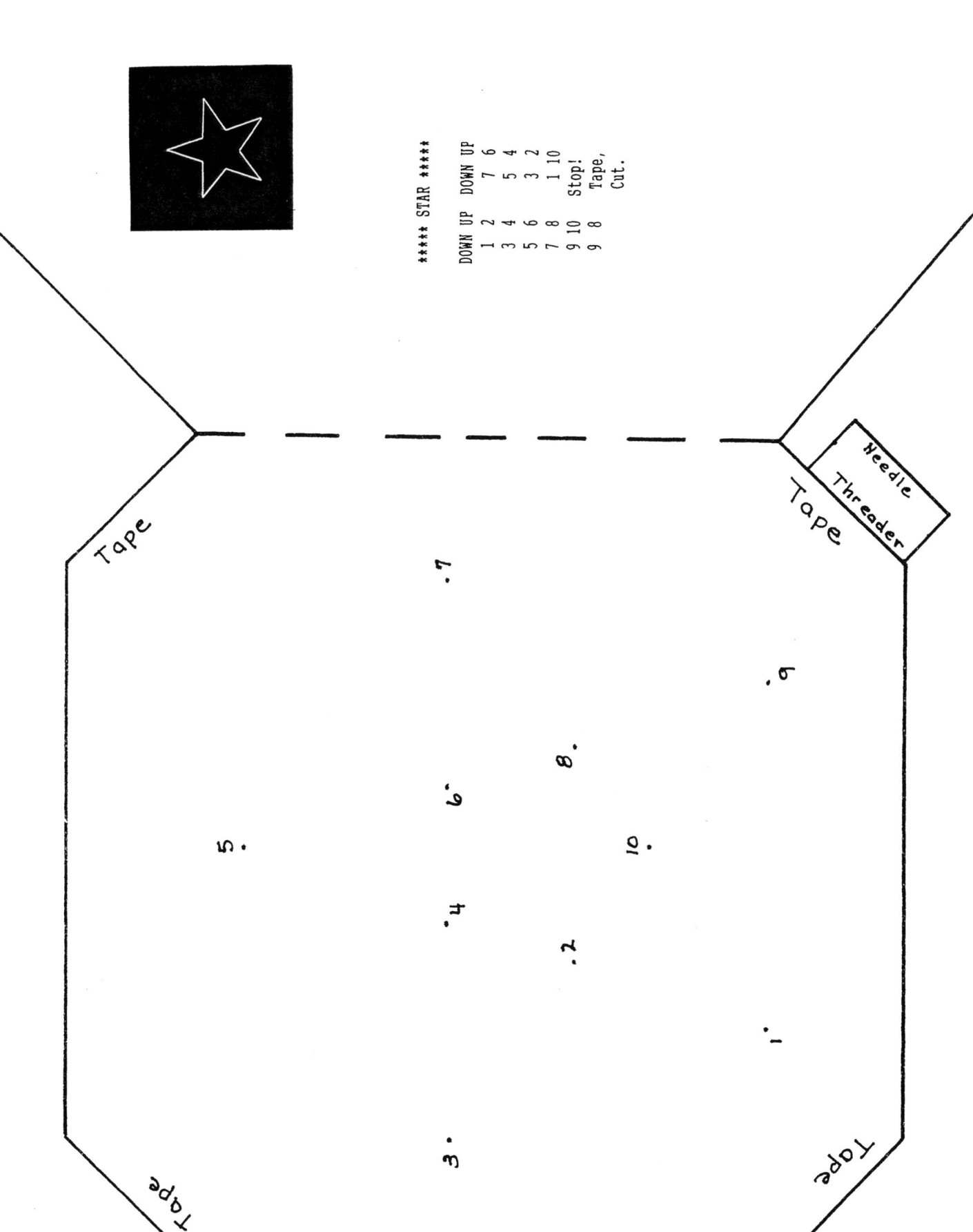

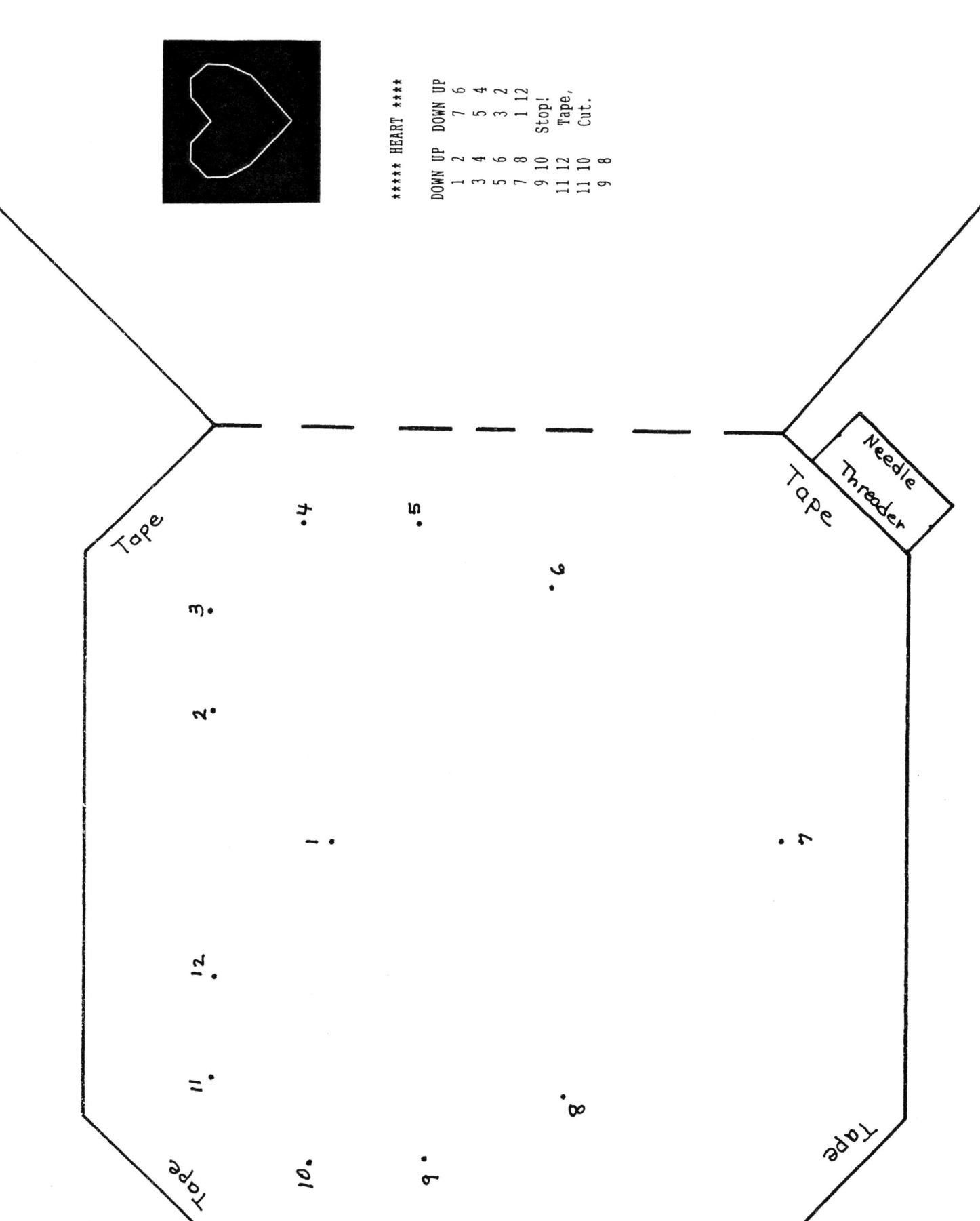

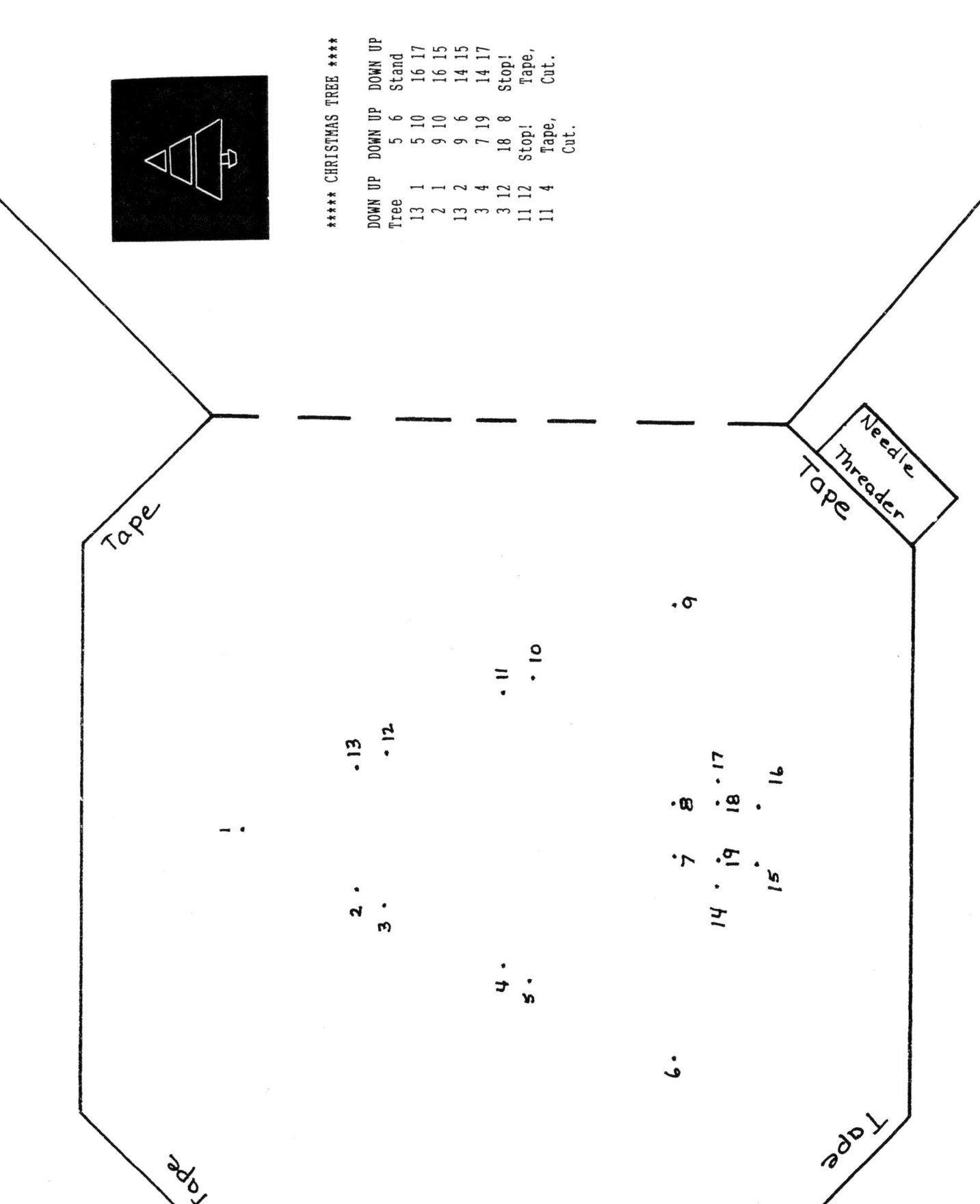

***** CHRISTMAS TREE ****

DOWN	UP	DOWN	UP	DOWN	UP
Tree				Stand	
13	1	5	6	16	17
2	1	5	10	16	15
13	2	9	10	14	15
3	4	9	6	14	17
3	12	7	19	Stop!	
11	12	18	8	Tape,	
11	4	Stop!		Cut.	
		Tape,			
		Cut.			

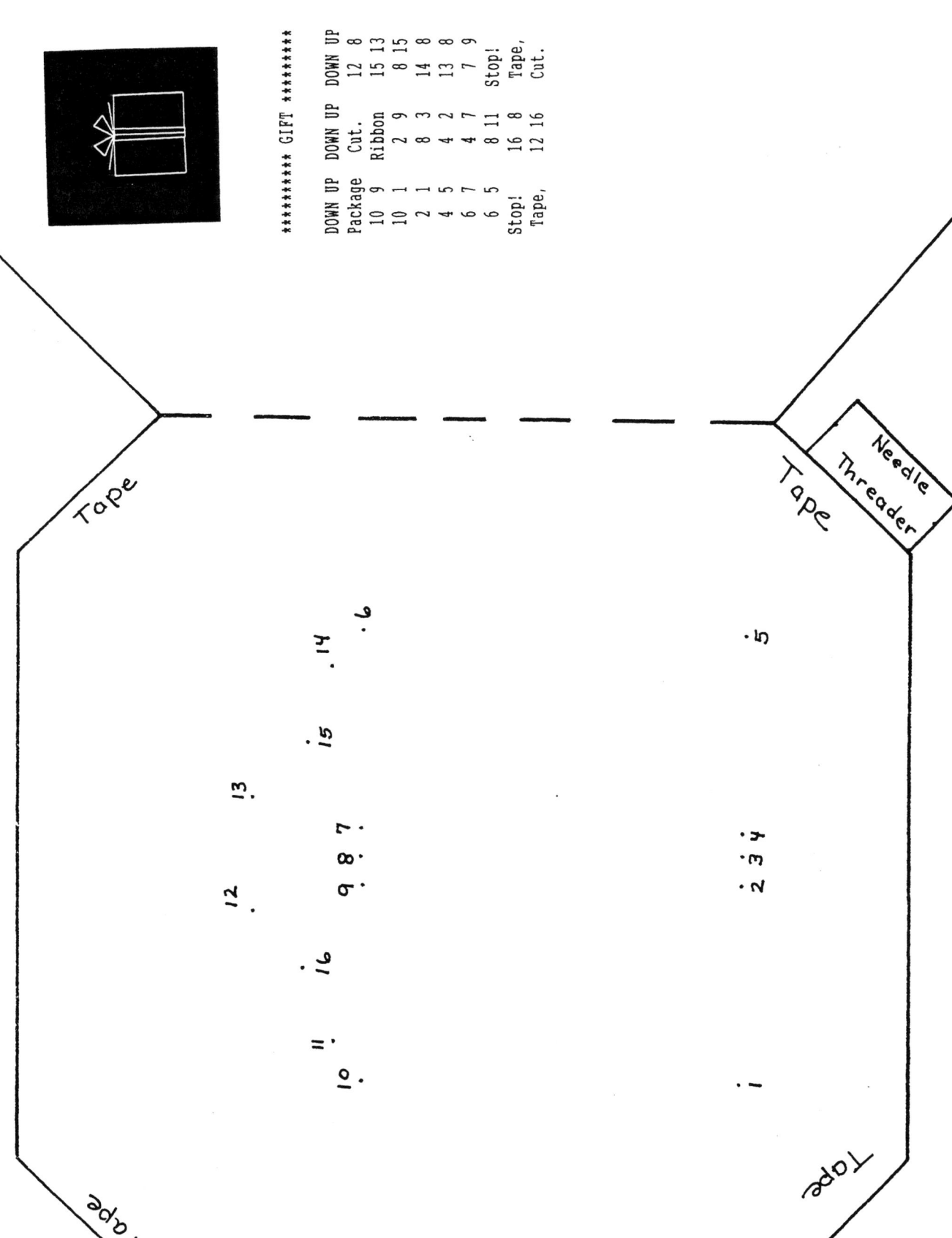

********** GIFT **********

DOWN	UP	DOWN	UP	DOWN	UP
Package		Cut.		12	8
10	9	Ribbon		15	13
10	1	2	9	8	15
2	1	8	3	14	8
4	5	4	2	13	8
6	7	4	7	7	9
6	5	8	11	Stop!	
Stop!		16	8	Tape,	
Tape,		12	16	Cut.	

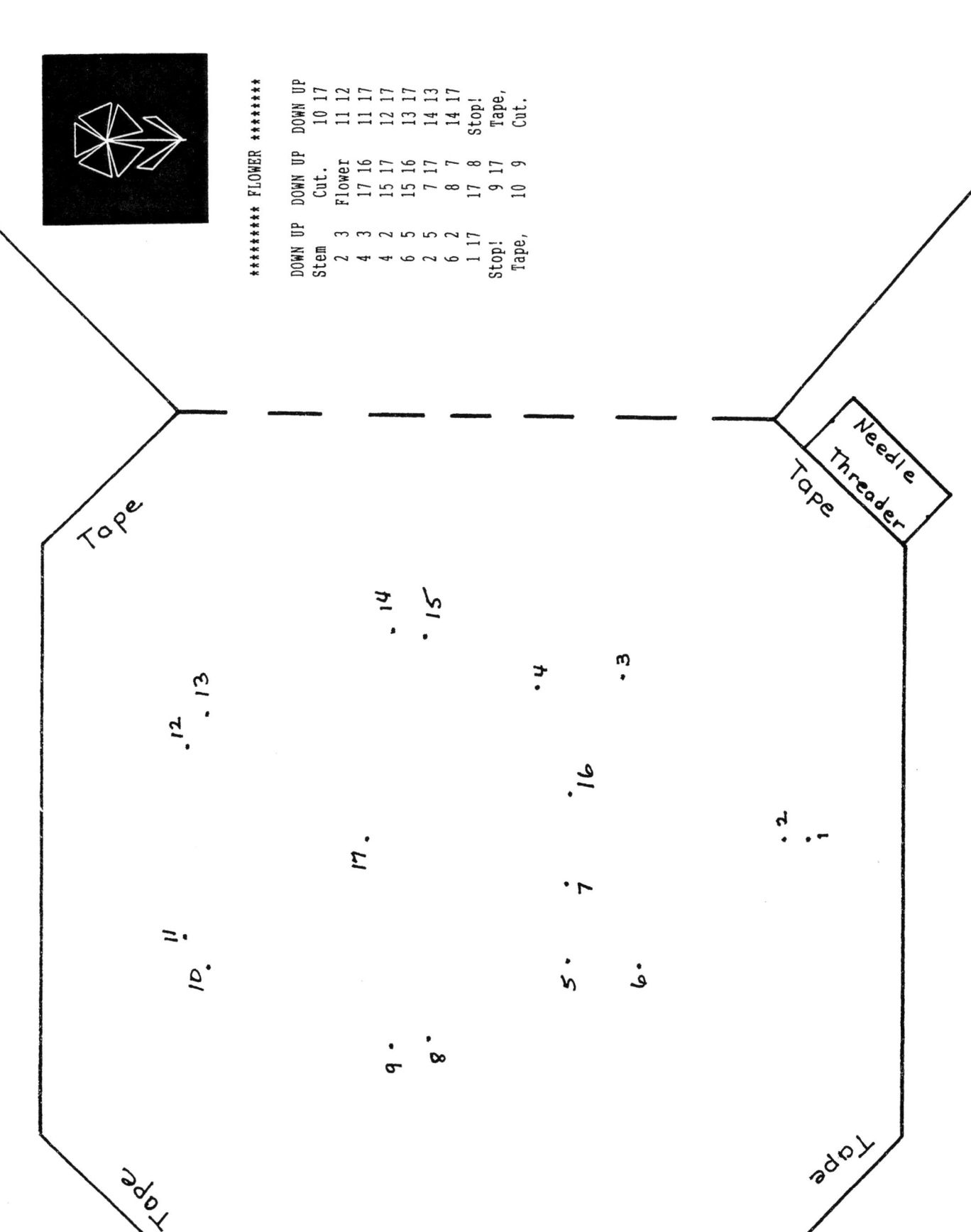

********** FLOWER **********

DOWN	UP	DOWN	UP	DOWN	UP
Stem		Cut.		10	17
2	3	Flower		11	12
4	3	17	16	11	17
4	2	15	17	12	17
6	5	15	16	13	17
2	5	7	17	14	13
6	2	8	7	14	17
1	17	17	8	Stop!	
Stop!		9	17	Tape,	
Tape,		10	9	Cut.	

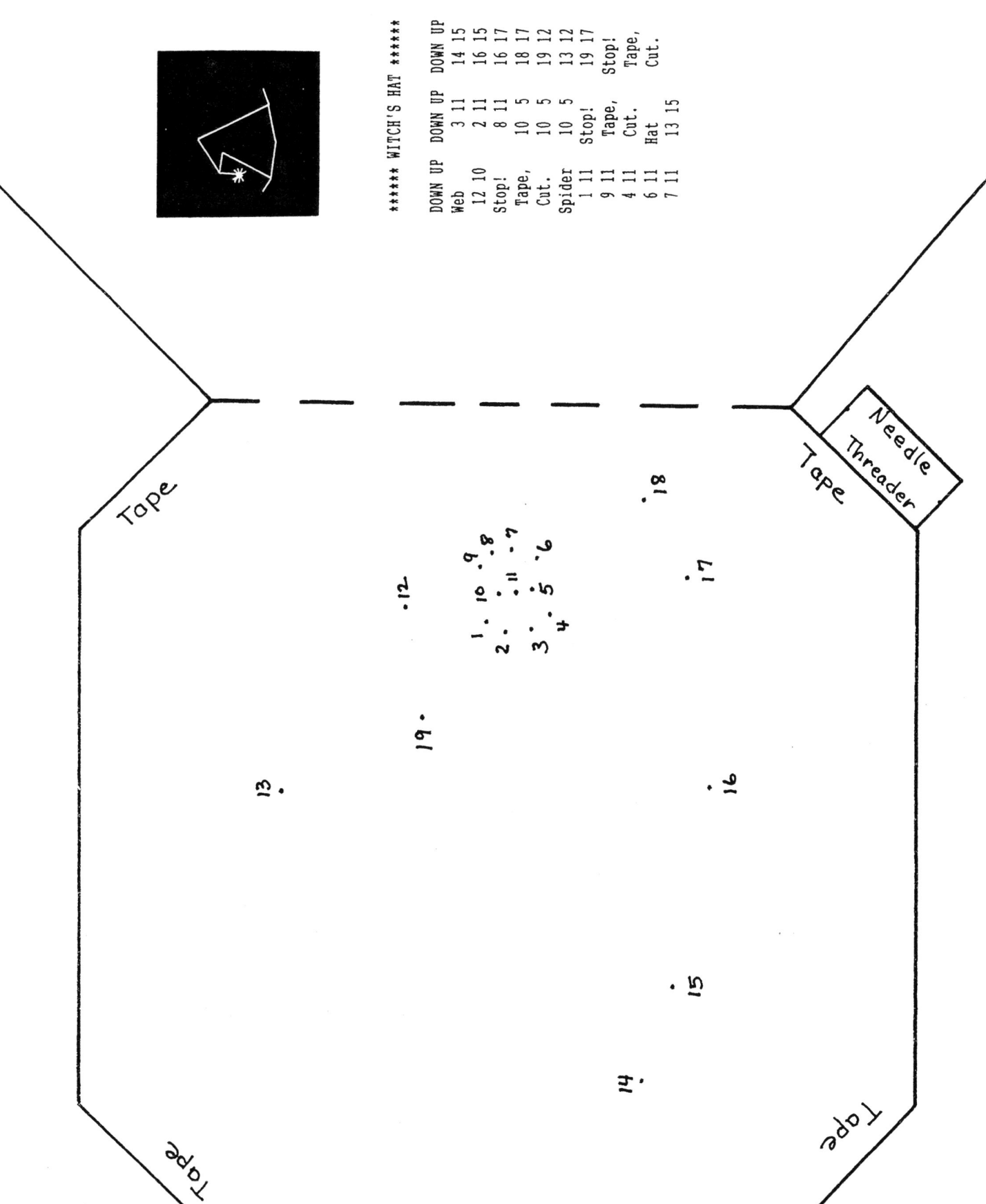

****** WITCH'S HAT ******

DOWN	UP	DOWN	UP	DOWN	UP
Web	3	11	14	15
12	10	2	11	16	15
Stop!	8	11	16	17
Tape,	10	5	18	17
Cut.	10	5	19	12
Spider	10	5	13	12
1	11	Stop!	19	17
9	11	Tape,	Stop!
4	11	Cut.	Tape,
6	11	Hat	Cut.
7	11	13	15

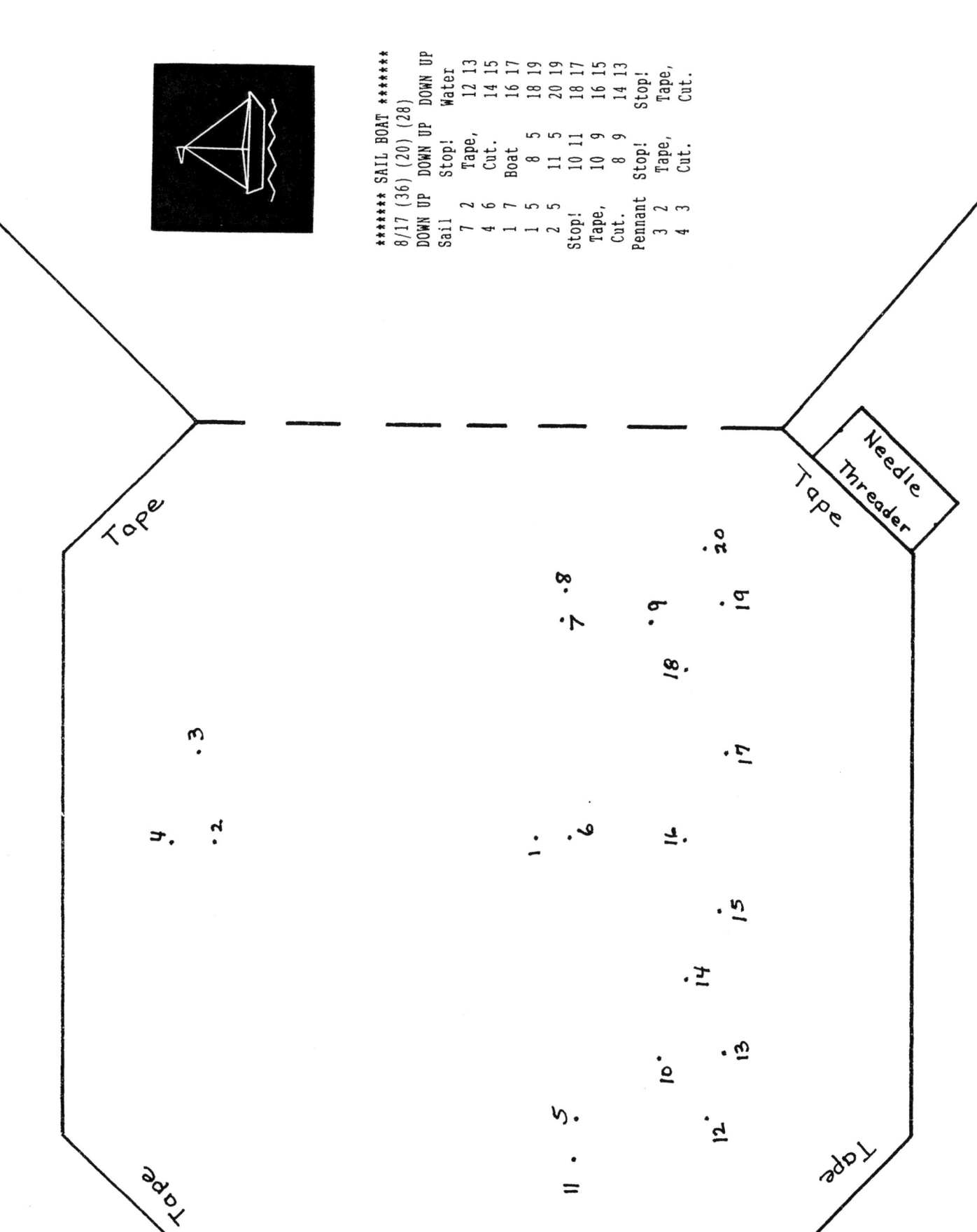

******** SAIL BOAT ********
8/17 (36) (20) (28)
DOWN UP DOWN UP DOWN UP
Sail   Stop!   Water
 7 2   Tape,   12 13
 4 6   Cut.   14 15
 1 7   Boat   16 17
 1 5   8 5   18 19
 2 5   11 5   20 19
Stop!   10 11   18 17
Tape,   10 9   16 15
Cut.   8 9   14 13
Pennant Stop!   Stop!
 3 2   Tape,   Tape,
 4 3   Cut.   Cut.

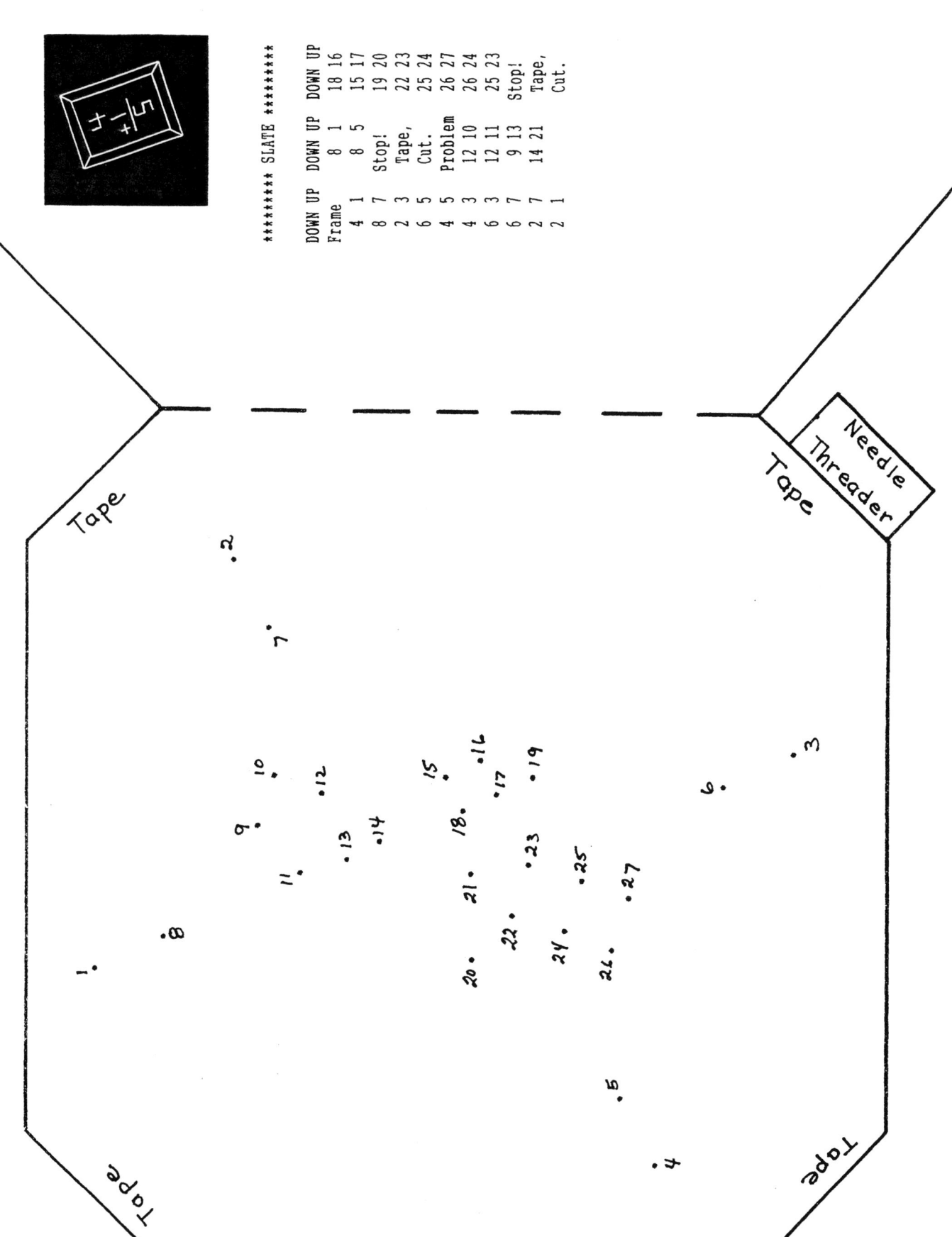

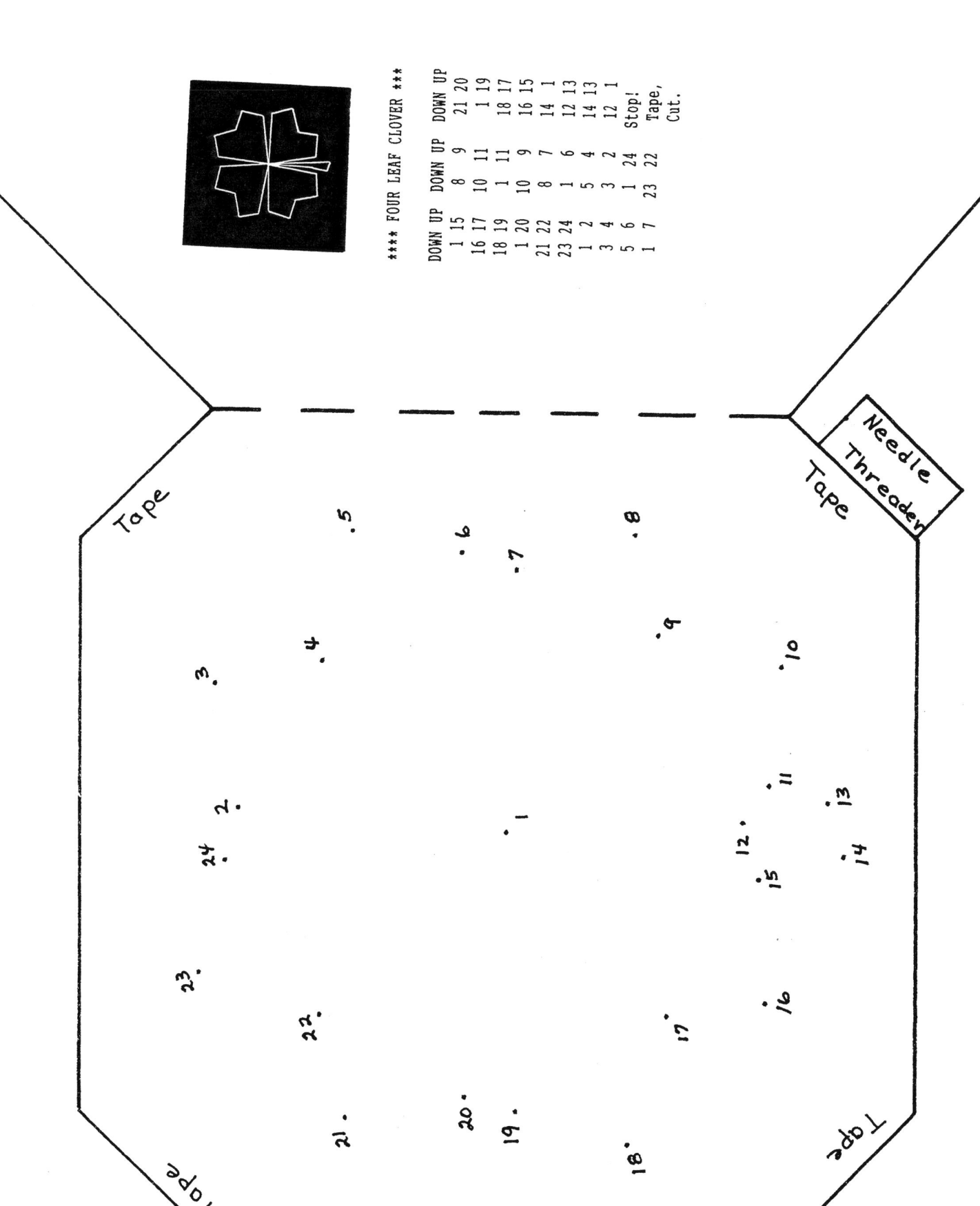

**** FOUR LEAF CLOVER ***

DOWN	UP	DOWN	UP	DOWN	UP
1	15	8	9	21	20
16	17	10	11	1	19
18	19	1	11	18	17
1	20	10	9	16	15
21	22	8	7	14	1
23	24	1	6	12	13
1	2	5	4	14	13
3	4	3	2	12	1
5	6	1	24	Stop!	
1	7	23	22	Tape,	
				Cut.	

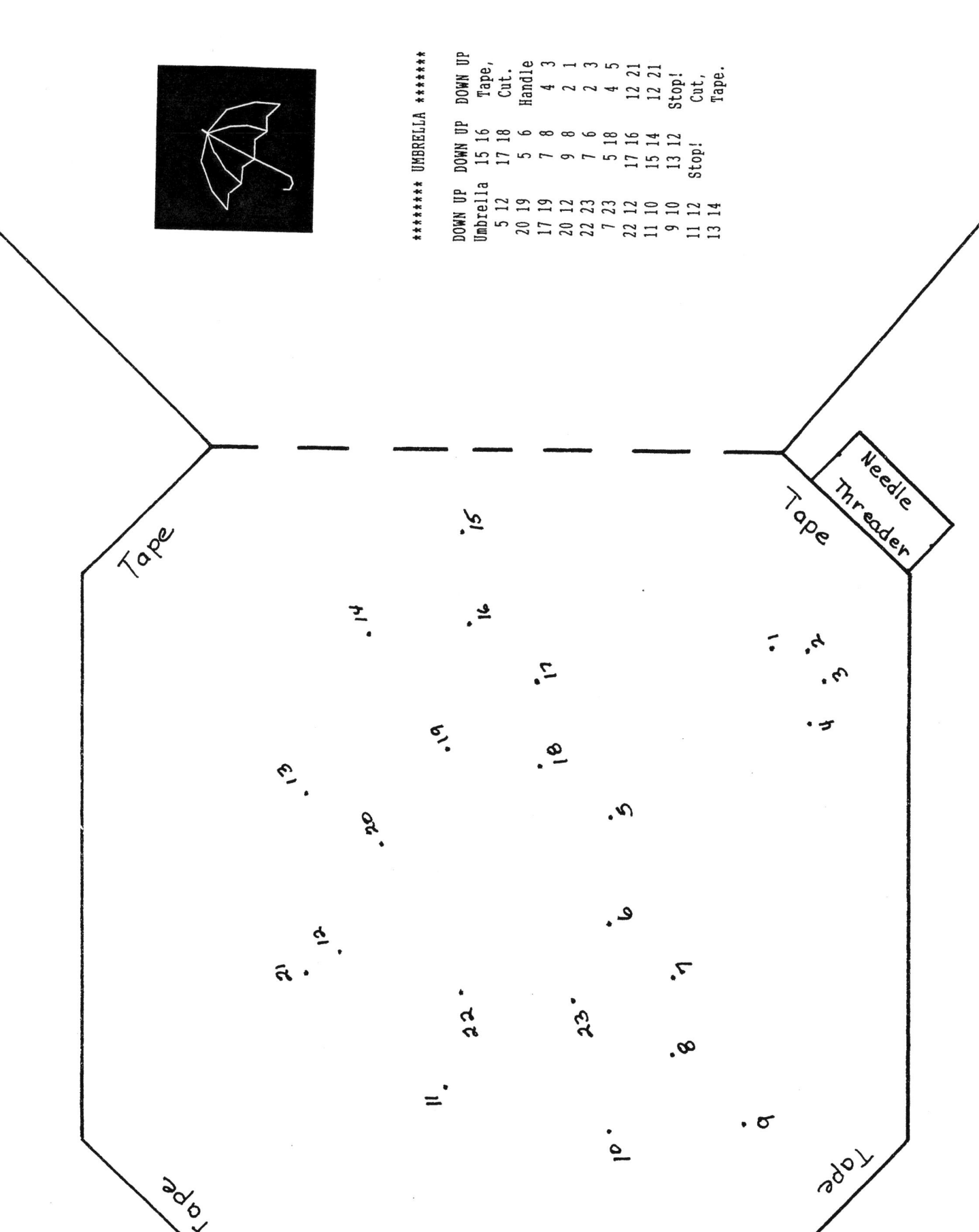

********* CRAYON **********

DOWN	UP	DOWN	UP	DOWN	UP
Crayon		7	8	10	3
1	2	9	10	10	11
1	12	9	4	2	11
11	12	3	4	13	18
Stop!		5	6	14	13
Tape,		7	6	18	17
Cut.		Stop!		16	15
7	19	Tape,		17	16
20	21	Cut.		15	14
22	23	Paper		Stop!	
22	21	wrap		Tape,	
20	19	2	3	Cut.	

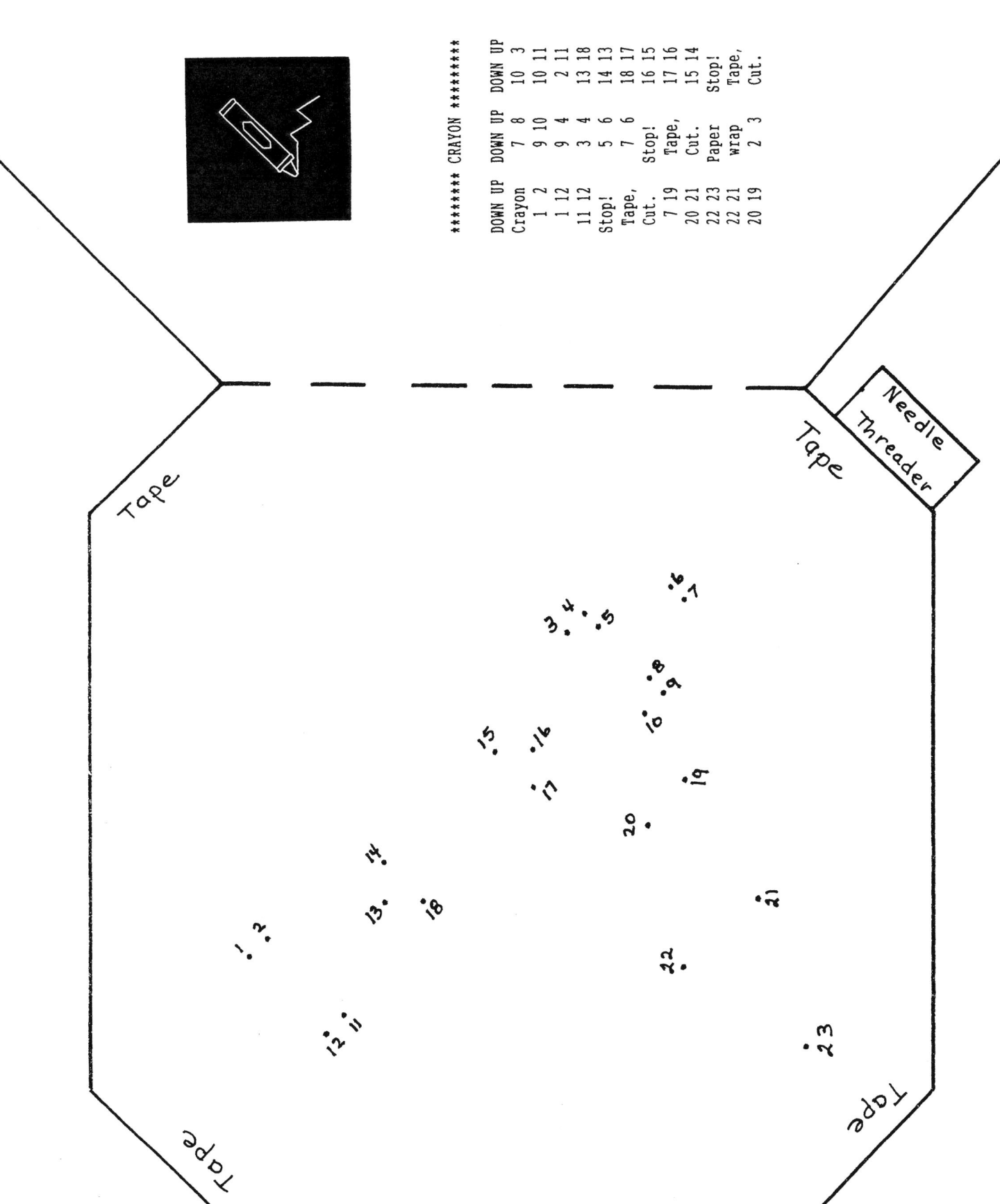

********** KITE **********

DOWN	UP	DOWN	UP	DOWN	UP
Kite		Tape,		2	3
8	11	Cut.		4	3
10	9	String		2	3
8	9	9	12	4	3
10	11	11	12	6	5
Stop!		13	14	6	7
Tape,		13	12	6	5
Cut.		Stop!		6	7
Tail		Tape,		6	5
6	3	Cut.		6	7
1	3	Ties		Stop!	
6	8	2	3	Tape,	
Stop!		4	3	Cut.	

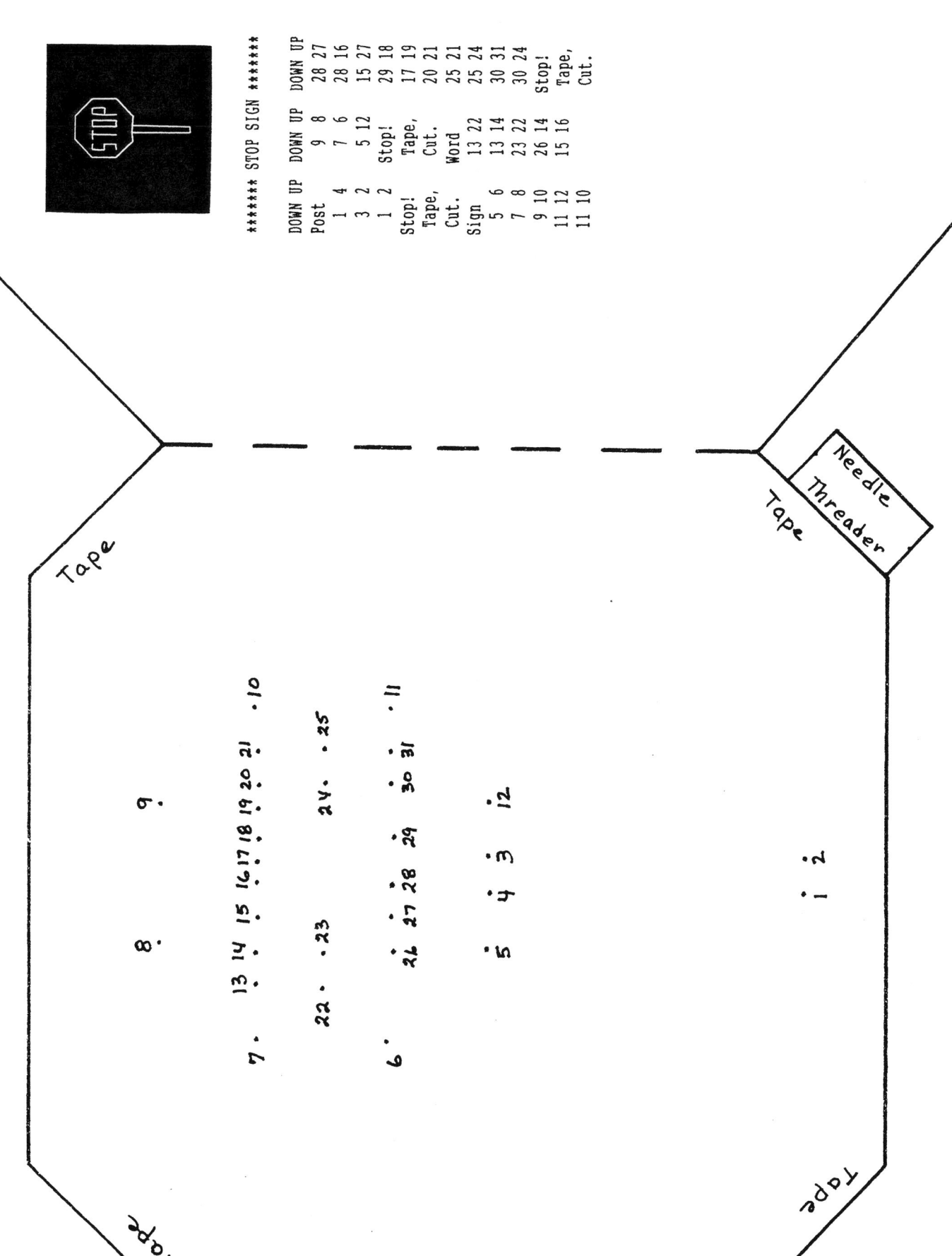

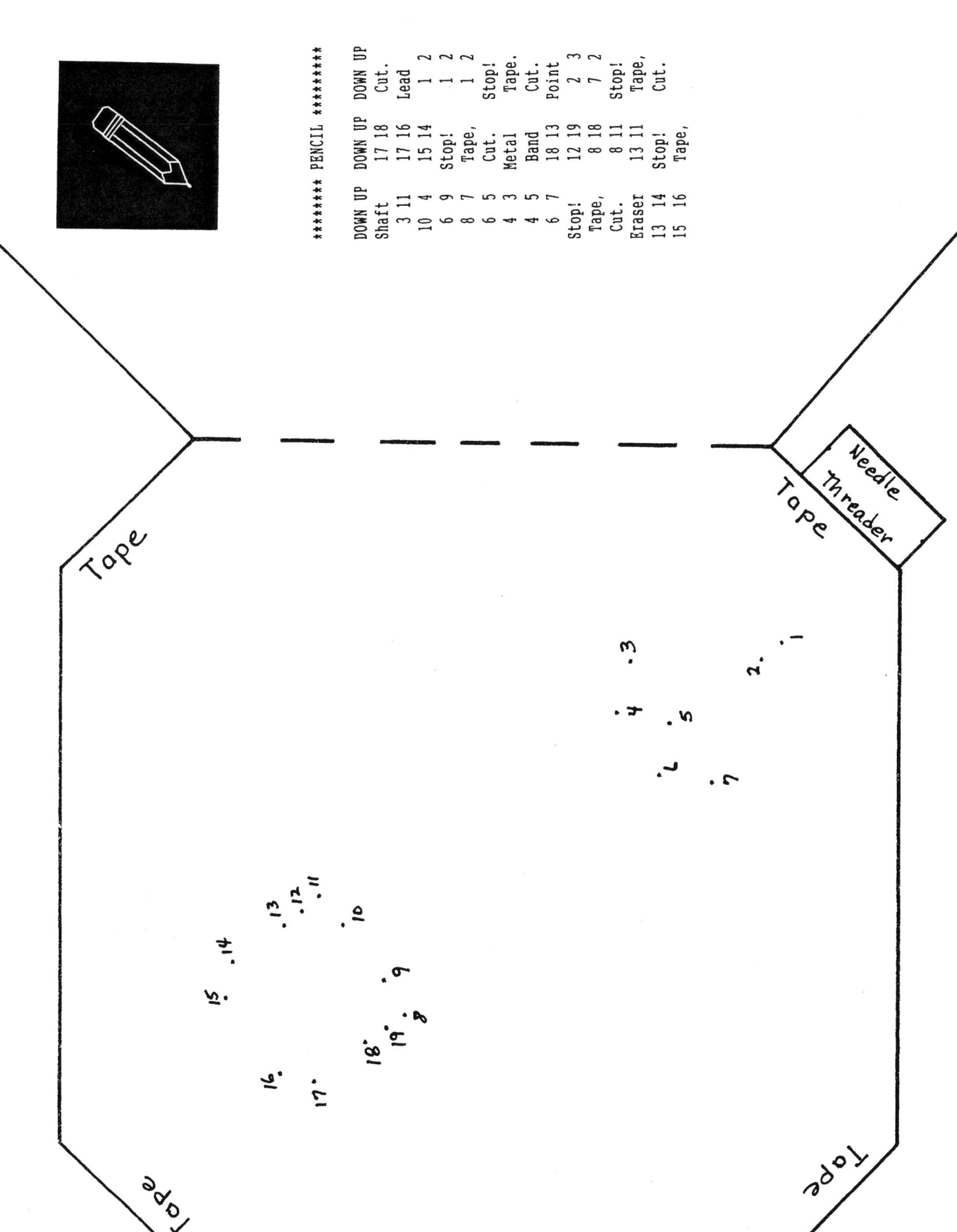

```
********* PENCIL *********
DOWN UP   DOWN UP   DOWN UP
Shaft     17 18     Cut.
3 11      17 16     Lead
10 4      15 14     Stop!    1 2
6 9       Stop!     Tape,    1 2
8 7       Tape,     Cut.     1 2
6 5       Cut.      Stop!
4 3       Metal     Tape.
4 5       Band      Cut.
6 7       18 13     Point
Stop!     12 19     2 3
Tape,     8 18      7 2
Cut.      8 11      Stop!
Eraser    13 11     Tape,
13 14     Stop!     Cut.
15 16     Tape,
```

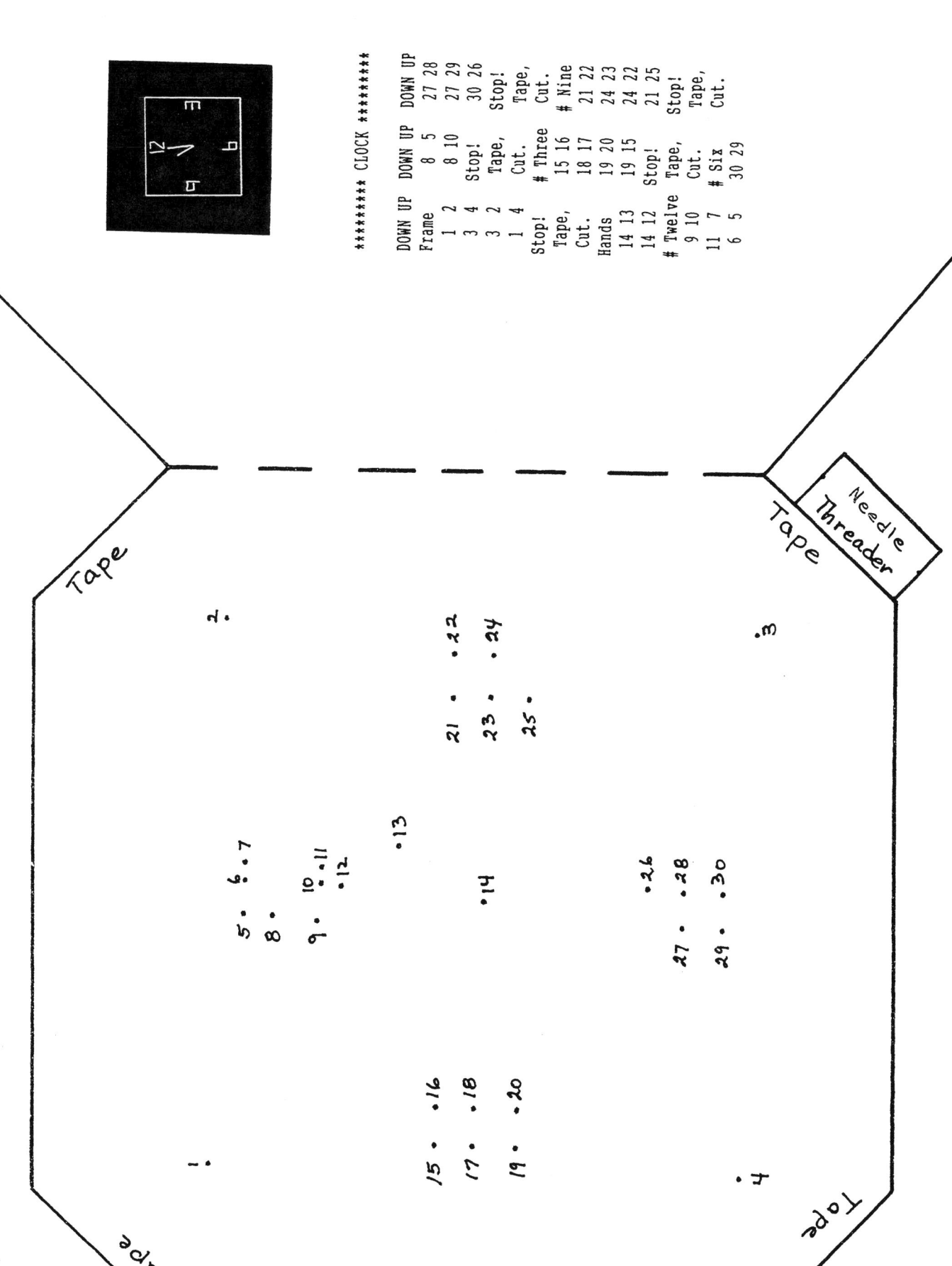

********** MITTEN **********

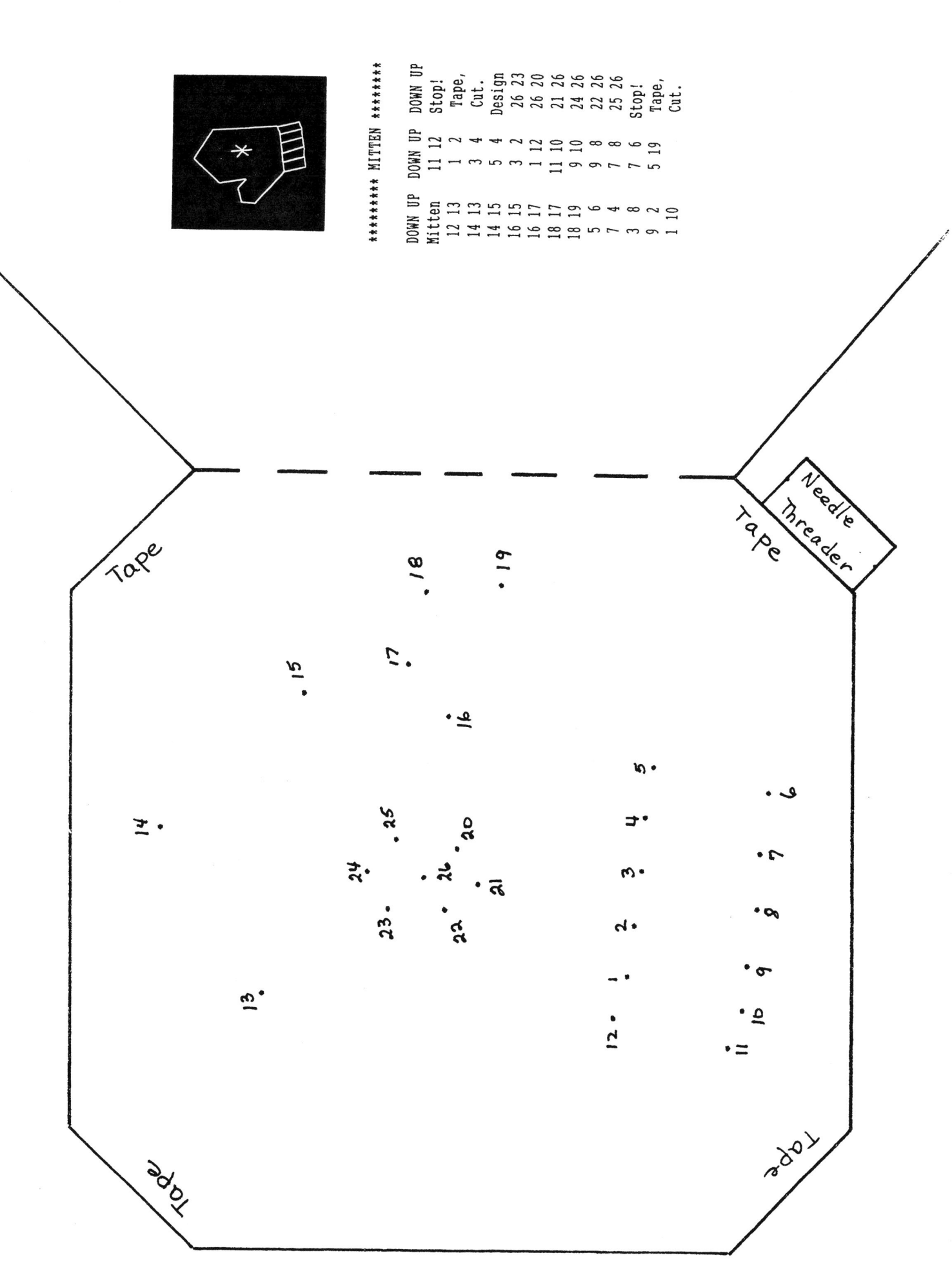

DOWN	UP	DOWN	UP	DOWN	UP
Mitten		11	12	Stop!	
12	13	1	2	Tape,	
14	13	3	4	Cut.	
14	15	5	4	Design	
16	15	3	2	26	23
16	17	1	12	26	20
18	17	11	10	21	26
18	19	9	10	24	26
5	6	9	8	22	26
7	4	7	8	25	26
3	8	7	6	Stop!	
9	2	5	19	Tape,	
1	10			Cut.	

Tape

Needle Threader

Tape

Tape

Tape

***** THIN BUTTERFLY *****

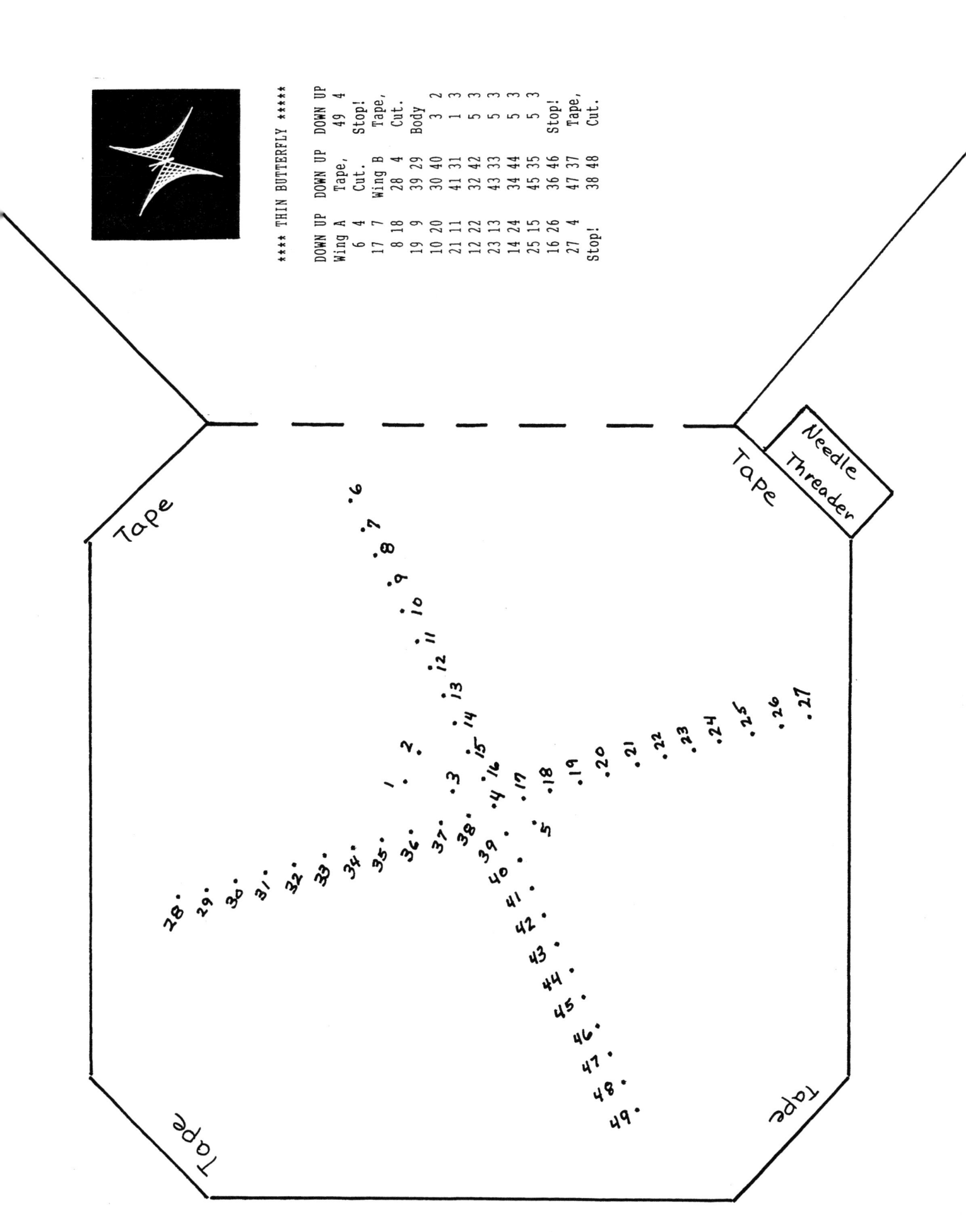

DOWN	UP	DOWN	UP	DOWN	UP
Wing A		Tape,		49	4
6	4	Cut.		Stop!	
17	7	Wing B		Tape,	
8	18	28	4	Cut.	
19	9	39	29	Body	
10	20	30	40	3	2
21	11	41	31	1	3
12	22	32	42	5	3
23	13	43	33	5	3
14	24	34	44	5	3
25	15	45	35	5	3
16	26	36	46	Stop!	
27	4	47	37	Tape,	
Stop!		38	48	Cut.	

******* ANGEL FISH ******

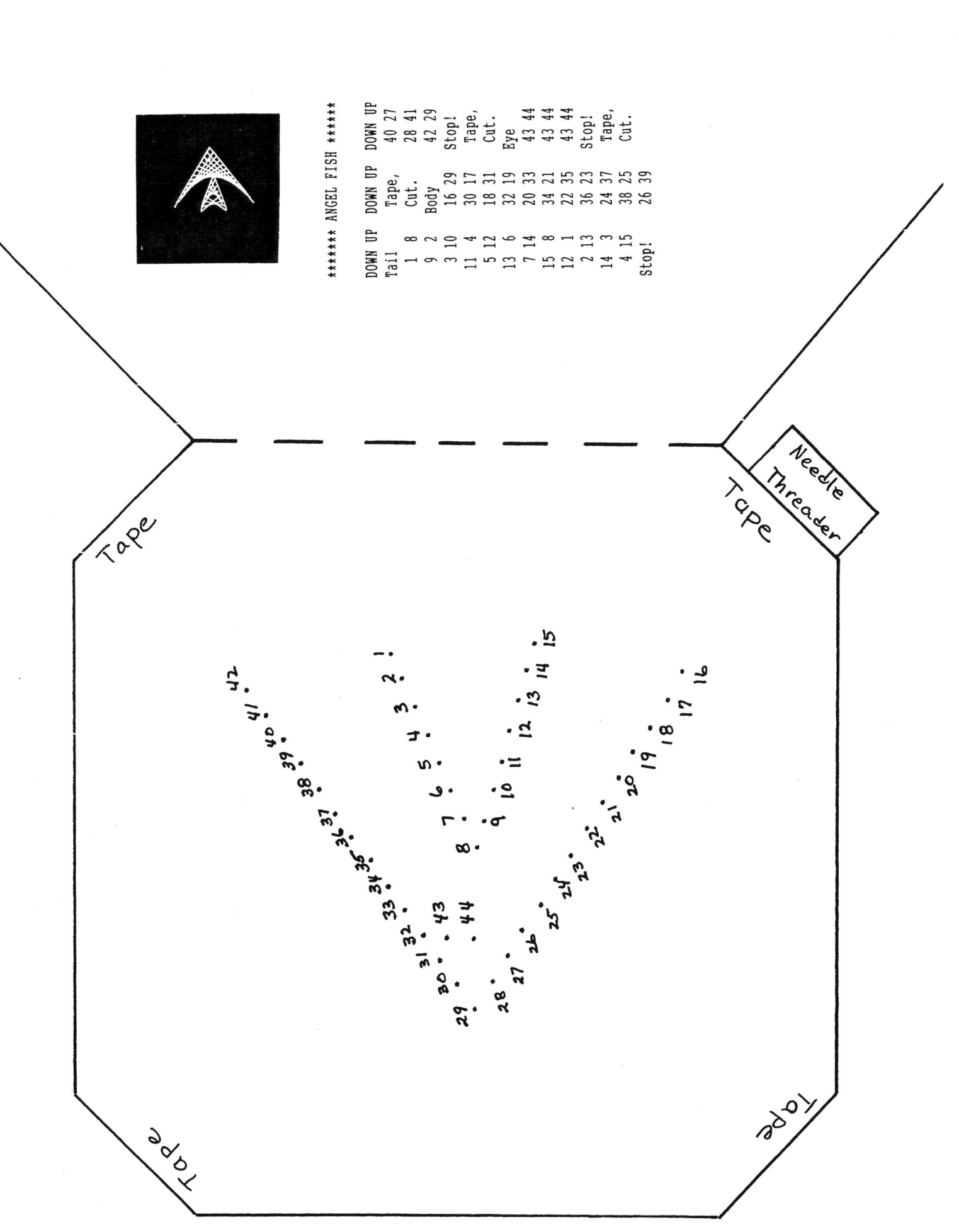

DOWN	UP	DOWN	UP	DOWN	UP
Tail		Tape,		40	27
1	8	Cut.		28	41
9	2	Body		42	29
3	10	16	29	Stop!	
11	4	30	17	Tape,	
5	12	18	31	Cut.	
13	6	32	19	Eye	
7	14	20	33	43	44
15	8	34	21	43	44
12	1	22	35	43	44
2	13	36	23	Stop!	
14	3	24	37	Tape,	
4	15	38	25	Cut.	
Stop!		26	39		

********** EGG **********

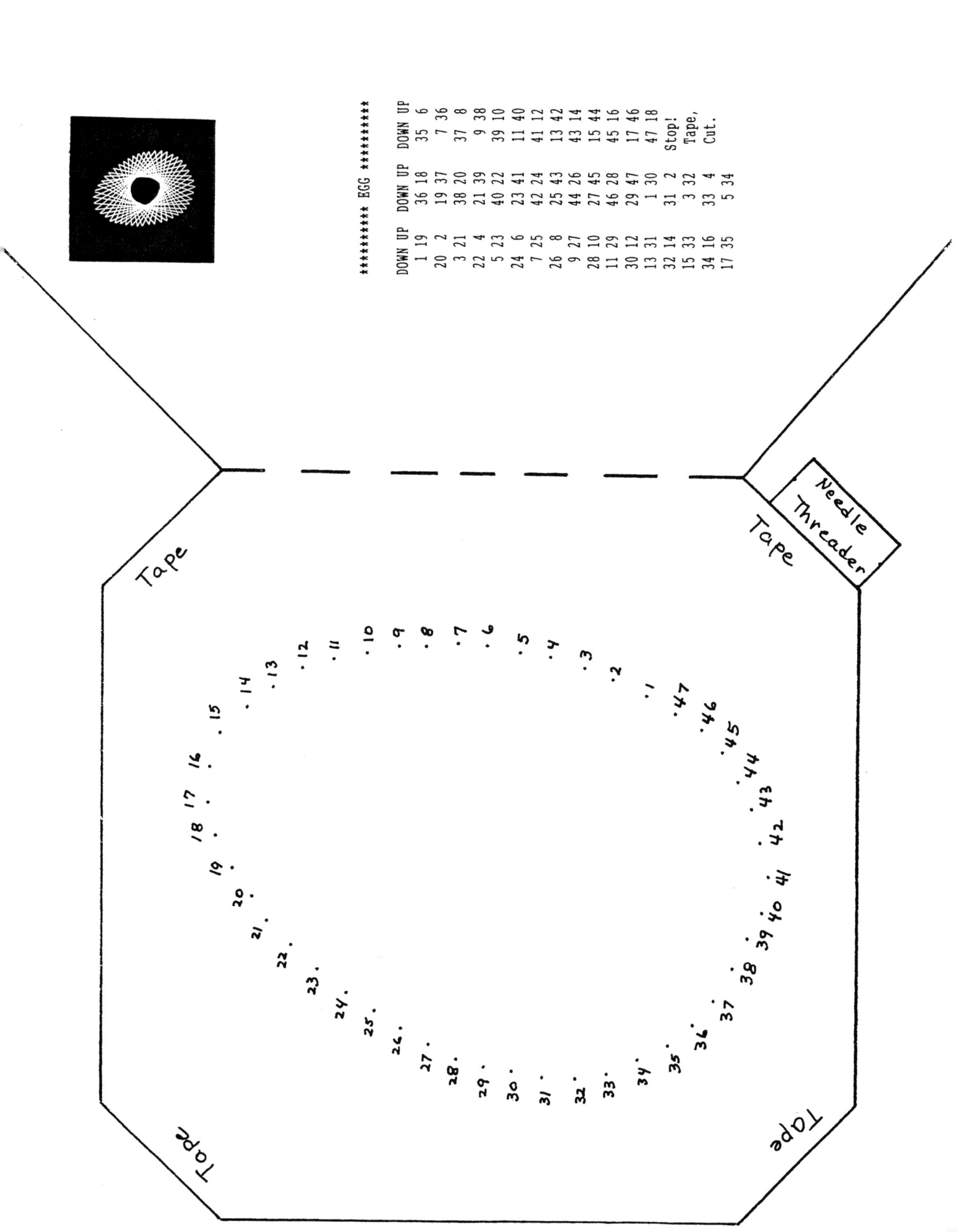

DOWN	UP	DOWN	UP	DOWN	UP
1	19	36	18	35	6
20	2	19	37	7	36
3	21	38	20	37	8
22	4	21	39	9	38
5	23	40	22	39	10
24	6	23	41	11	40
7	25	42	24	41	12
26	8	25	43	13	42
9	27	44	26	43	14
28	10	27	45	15	44
11	29	46	28	45	16
30	12	29	47	17	46
13	31	1	30	47	18
32	14	31	2	Stop!	
15	33	3	32	Tape,	
34	16	33	4	Cut.	
17	35	5	34		

Tape

Tape

Needle Threader

Tape

Tape

** ICE CREAM IN A CONE **

DOWN	UP	DOWN	UP	DOWN	UP
Cone		Cut.		7	26
34	43	Ice Cream		27	8
42	43	22	10	9	28
42	39	11	23	29	10
41	32	24	12	11	30
31	33	13	25	31	12
35	29	26	14	13	1
27	36	15	27	2	14
37	25	28	16	15	3
23	38	17	29	4	16
40	38	30	18	17	5
37	36	19	31	6	18
35	33	1	20	19	7
35	36	21	2	8	20
37	38	3	22	21	9
40	21	23	4	Stop!	
Stop!		5	24	Tape,	
Tape,		25	6	Cut.	

********* TEPEE *********

DOWN	UP	DOWN	UP	DOWN	UP
POLES		5	55	19	37
33	57	56	51	38	20
58	33	56	5	21	39
61	33	6	12	40	22
60	33	11	5	23	41
59	33	7	13	42	24
Stop!		14	8	25	43
Tape,		9	15	44	26
Cut.		16	10	27	45
Tee Pee		11	17	46	28
46	52	18	12	29	47
53	47	13	19	48	30
48	54	20	14	31	49
55	49	15	10	50	32
50	56	5	10	33	51
1	51	15	33	Stop!	
52	2	34	16	Tape,	
3	53	17	35	Cut.	
54	4	36	18		

********** DONUT **********

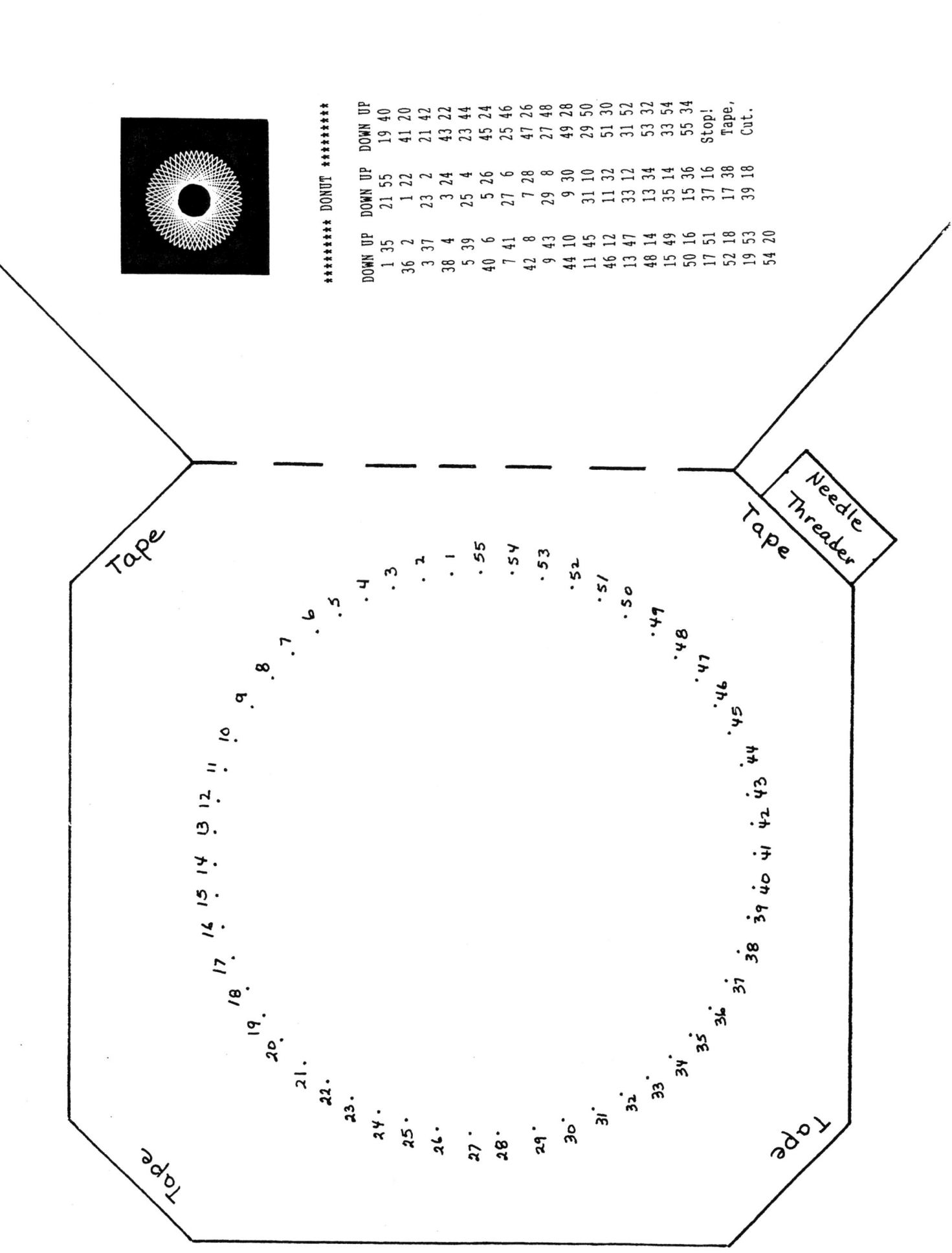

DOWN	UP	DOWN	UP	DOWN	UP
1	35	21	55	19	40
36	2	1	22	41	20
3	37	23	2	21	42
38	4	3	24	43	22
5	39	25	4	23	44
40	6	5	26	45	24
7	41	27	6	25	46
42	8	7	28	47	26
9	43	29	8	27	48
44	10	9	30	49	28
11	45	31	10	29	50
46	12	11	32	51	30
13	47	33	12	31	52
48	14	13	34	53	32
15	49	35	14	33	54
50	16	15	36	55	34
17	51	37	16	Stop!	
52	18	17	38	Tape,	
19	53	39	18	Cut.	
54	20				

********** PEAR **********

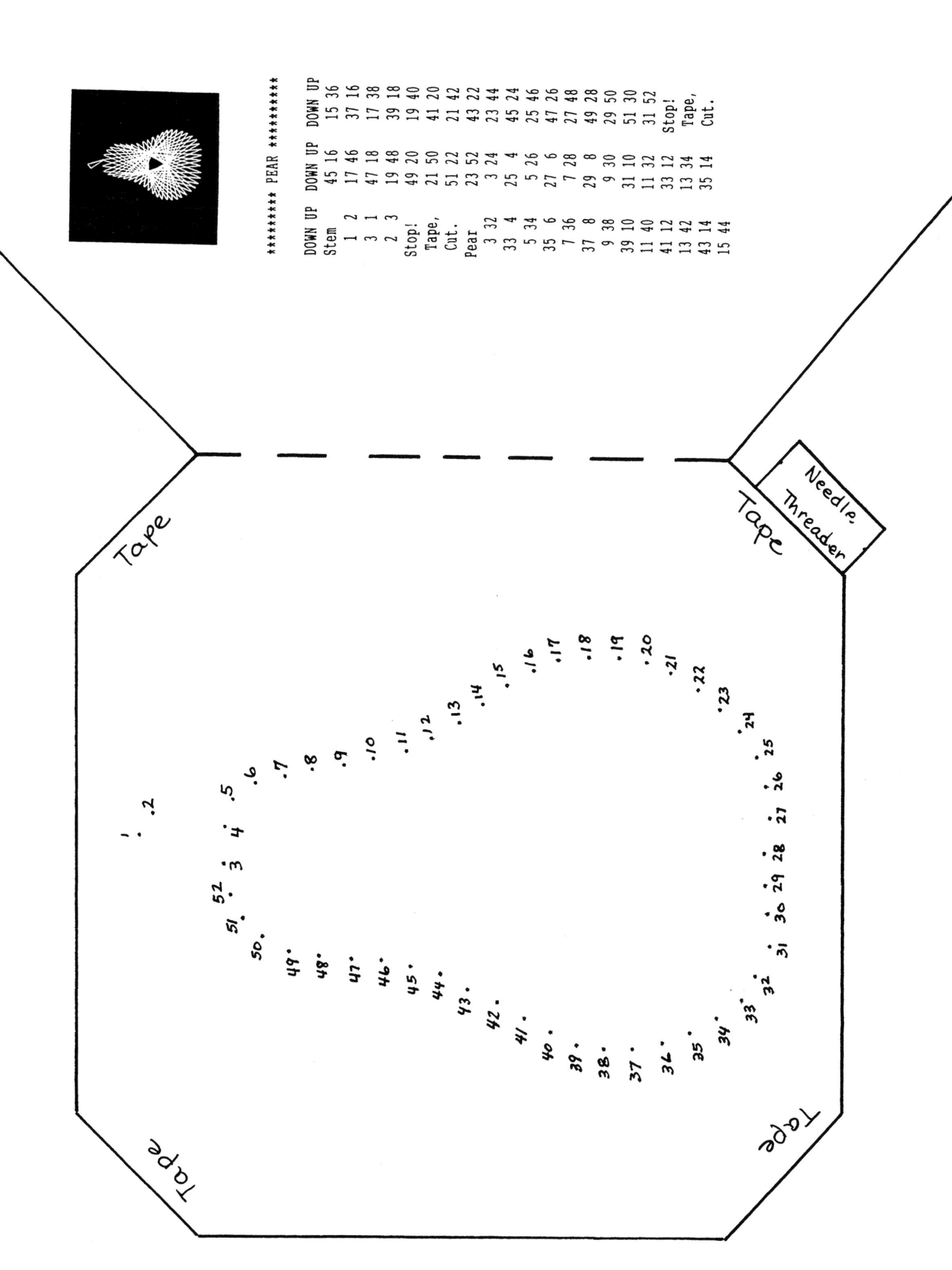

DOWN	UP	DOWN	UP	DOWN	UP
Stem		45	16	15	36
1	2	17	46	37	16
3	1	47	18	17	38
2	3	19	48	39	18
Stop!		49	20	19	40
Tape,		21	50	41	20
Cut.		51	22	21	42
Pear		23	52	43	22
3	32	3	24	23	44
33	4	25	4	45	24
5	34	5	26	25	46
35	6	27	6	47	26
7	36	7	28	27	48
37	8	29	8	49	28
9	38	9	30	29	50
39	10	31	10	51	30
11	40	11	32	31	52
41	12	33	12	Stop!	
13	42	13	34	Tape,	
43	14	35	14	Cut.	
15	44				

************ U S FLAG ************

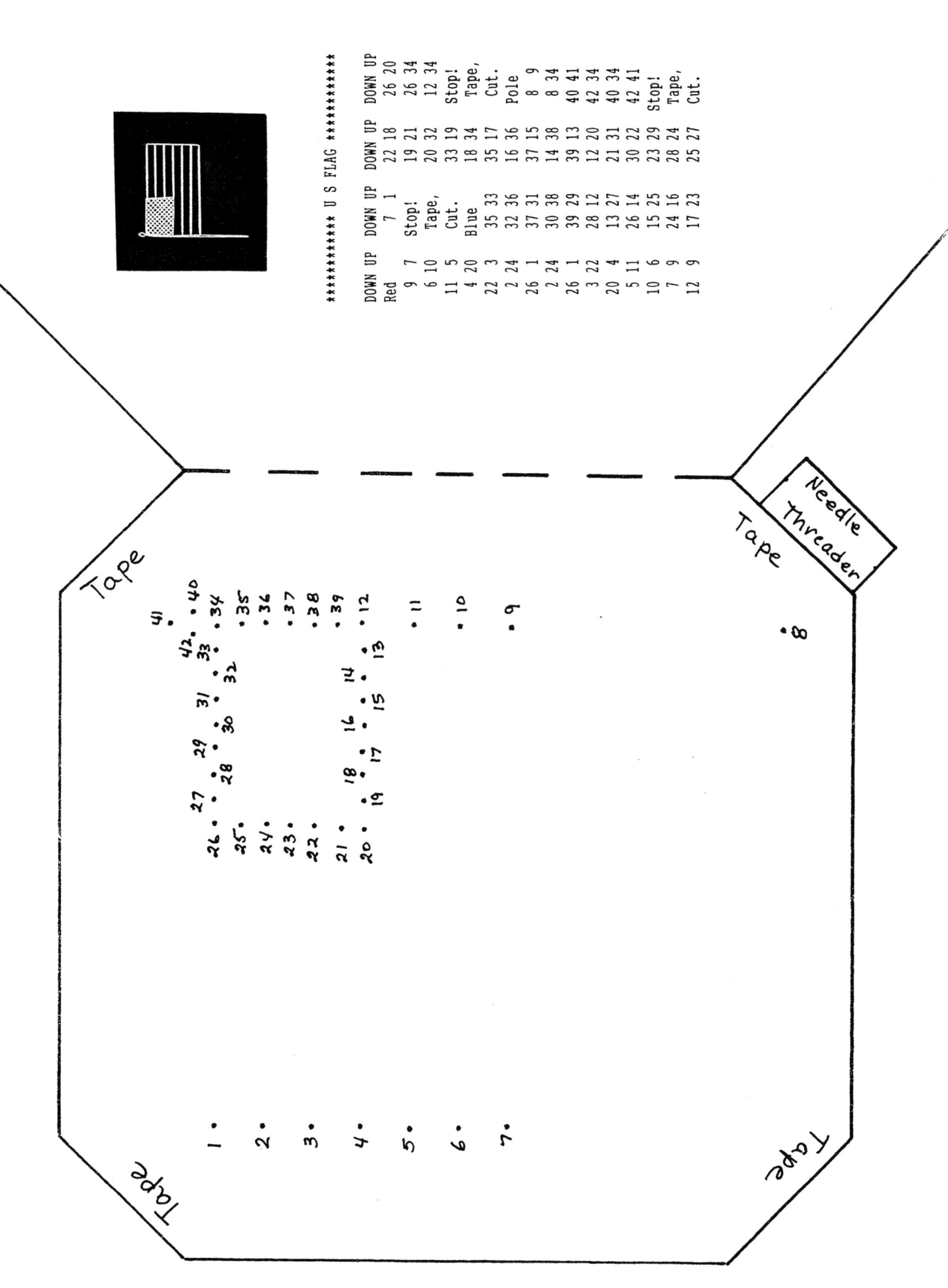

DOWN	UP	DOWN	UP	DOWN	UP	DOWN	UP
Red							
9	7	Stop!		22	18	26	20
6	10	Tape,		19	21	26	34
11	5	Cut.		20	32	12	34
4	20	Blue		33	19	Stop!	
22	3	35	33	18	34	Tape,	
2	24	32	36	35	17	Cut.	
26	1	37	31	16	36	Pole	
2	24	30	38	37	15	8	9
26	1	39	29	14	38	8	34
3	22	28	12	39	13	40	41
20	4	13	27	12	20	42	34
5	11	26	14	21	31	40	34
10	6	15	25	30	22	42	41
7	9	24	16	23	29	Stop!	
12	9	17	23	28	24	Tape,	
				25	27	Cut.	

********** TIE **********

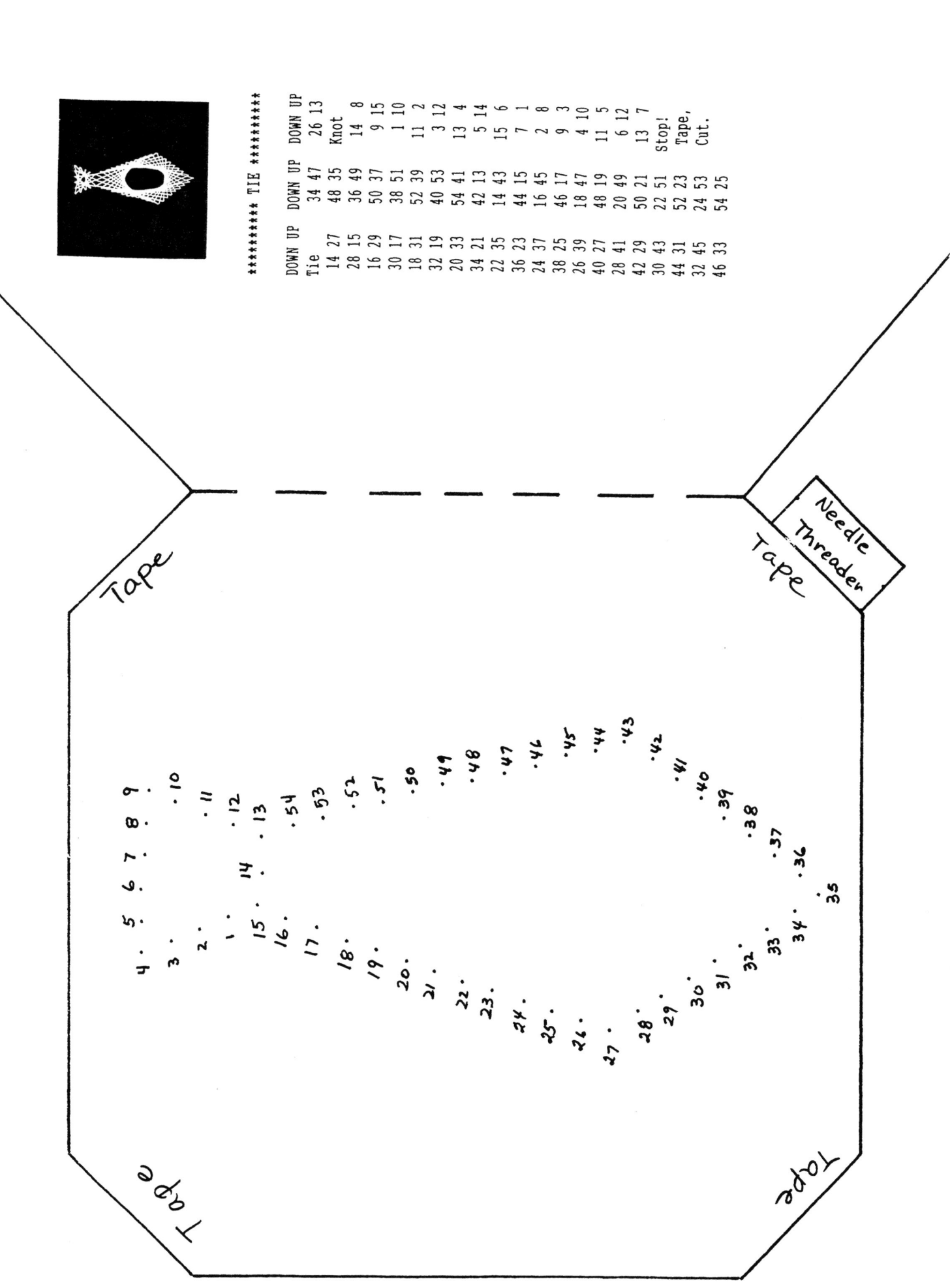

DOWN UP	DOWN UP	DOWN UP
Tie	34 47	26 13
14 27	48 35	Knot
28 15	36 49	14 8
16 29	50 37	9 15
30 17	38 51	1 10
18 31	52 39	11 2
32 19	40 53	3 12
20 33	54 41	13 4
34 21	42 13	5 14
22 35	14 43	15 6
36 23	44 15	7 1
24 37	16 45	2 8
38 25	46 17	9 3
26 39	18 47	4 10
40 27	48 19	11 5
28 41	20 49	6 12
42 29	50 21	13 7
30 43	22 51	Stop!
44 31	52 23	Tape,
32 45	24 53	Cut.
46 33	54 25	

Tape

Tape

Needle Threader

Tape

Tape

***** SPRING FLOWER *****

DOWN	UP	DOWN	UP	DOWN	UP
Leaves		36	56	10	30
& Stem		57	37	31	11
1	2	38	10	12	32
3	4	11	39	33	13
5	4	40	12	14	34
3	2	13	41	35	15
9	8	42	14	16	36
7	5	15	43	37	17
1	9	44	16	18	38
8	7	17	45	39	19
6	10	46	18	20	40
Stop!		19	47	41	21
Tape,		48	20	22	42
Cut.		21	49	43	23
Flower		50	22	24	44
49	29	23	51	45	25
30	50	52	24	46	26
51	31	25	53	47	27
32	52	54	26	28	48
53	33	27	55	Stop!	
34	54	56	28	Tape,	
55	35	29	57	Cut.	

* CHRISTMAS DECORATION **

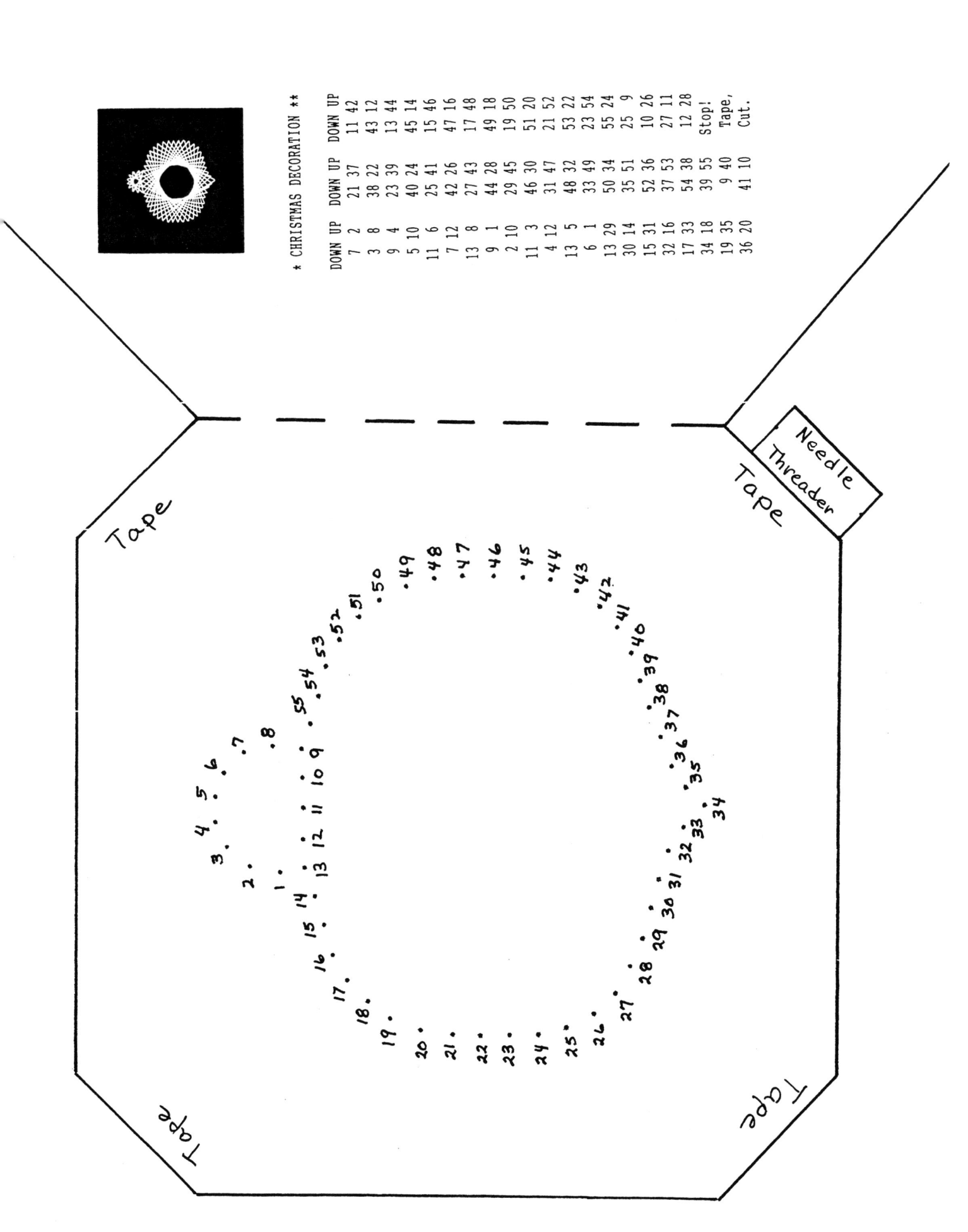

DOWN	UP	DOWN	UP	DOWN	UP
7	2	21	37	11	42
3	8	38	22	43	12
9	4	23	39	13	44
5	10	40	24	45	14
11	6	25	41	15	46
7	12	42	26	47	16
13	8	27	43	17	48
9	1	44	28	49	18
2	10	29	45	19	50
11	3	46	30	51	20
4	12	31	47	21	52
13	5	48	32	53	22
6	1	33	49	23	54
13	29	50	34	55	24
30	14	35	51	25	9
15	31	52	36	10	26
32	16	37	53	27	11
17	33	54	38	12	28
34	18	39	55	Stop!	
19	35	9	40	Tape,	
36	20	41	10	Cut.	

*** FLOWERS IN A POT ***

DOWN	UP	DOWN	UP	DOWN	UP
Stems		Flower A		40	29
8	54	54	45	41	29
56	8	46	54	30	29
55	8	47	54	31	29
9	28	48	54	32	29
9	27	49	54	Stop!	
29	9	50	54	Tape,	
10	26	51	54	Cut.	
25	10	52	54	Flower C	
12	10	53	54	25	20
Stop!		42	54	21	25
Tape,		43	54	22	25
Cut.		44	54	23	25
Pot		Stop!		24	25
5	1	Tape,		13	25
2	1	Cut.		14	25
2	4	Flower B		15	25
3	11	29	33	16	25
3	6	34	29	17	25
7	6	35	29	18	25
7	11	36	29	19	25
Stop!		37	29	Stop!	
Tape,		38	29	Tape,	
Cut.		39	29	Cut.	

```
************ BALLOON ************

DOWN UP    DOWN UP    DOWN UP    DOWN UP
Balloon    34  55     23  53     11  15
38  17     56  35     54  24     16  12
18  39     36  57     25  55     13   7
40  19     58  37     56  26      8  14
20  41     38  59     27  57     15   9
42  21     60  39     58  28     10  16
22  43     40  61     29  59     Stop!
44  23     62  41     31  61     Tape,
24  45     42  63     60  30     Cut.
46  25     64  43     62  32     String
26  47     44  65     33  63      6   5
48  27     66  45     64  34      4   3
28  49     46  16     35  65      2   1
50  29     17  47     66  36      2   3
30  51     48  18     37  16      4   5
52  31     19  49      7  11      6  16
32  53     50  20     12   8     Stop!
54  33     21  51      9  13     Tape,
           52  22     14  10     Cut.
```

****** ICE CREAM ON A STICK ******

DOWN	UP	DOWN	UP	DOWN	UP	DOWN	UP
Stick		8	9	46	28	18	46
2	8	8	7	29	47	47	19
9	3	Stop!		48	30	20	48
4	10	Tape,		31	49	49	21
11	5	Cut.		50	32	22	50
6	12	Ice Cream		33	51	51	23
13	7	15	33	52	34	24	52
8	14	34	16	35	53	53	25
15	9	17	35	54	36	26	54
10	16	36	18	37	55	55	27
17	11	19	37	56	38	28	56
12	1	38	20	39	57	57	29
2	13	21	39	58	40	30	58
14	3	40	22	41	59	59	31
4	15	23	41	60	42	32	60
16	5	42	24	43	15	Stop!	
6	17	25	43	16	44	Tape,	
1	7	44	26	45	17	Cut.	
6	7	27	45				

********* CHRISTMAS LIGHT *********

DOWN	UP	DOWN	UP	DOWN	UP	DOWN	UP
Base		3	19	32	48	25	51
10	1	20	4	49	33	52	26
2	11	5	21	34	50	27	53
12	3	22	6	51	35	54	28
4	13	7	23	36	52	29	55
14	5	24	8	53	37	56	30
6	15	9	25	38	54	31	57
16	7	Stop!		55	39	58	32
8	17	Tape,		40	56	33	59
18	9	Cut.		57	41	60	34
10	19	Bulb		42	58	35	19
20	11	24	40	59	43	20	36
12	21	41	25	44	60	37	21
22	13	26	42	19	45	22	38
14	23	43	27	46	20	39	23
24	15	28	44	21	47	Stop!	
16	25	45	29	48	22	Tape,	
1	17	30	46	23	49	Cut.	
18	2	47	31	50	24		

************* FOOTBALL ************

DOWN	UP	DOWN	UP	DOWN	UP
Lacings	25 44	63 44	63 22
10 1	45 26	45 64	23 64
2 18	27 46	65 46	65 24
17 3	47 28	47 66	25 66
4 16	29 48	67 48	67 26
15 5	49 30	49 68	27 68
6 14	31 50	69 50	69 28
13 7	51 32	51 70	29 70
8 12	33 52	71 52	71 30
11 9	53 34	53 72	31 72
Stop!	35 54	73 54	73 32
Tape,	55 36	55 74	33 74
Cut.	37 56	75 56	75 34
Ball	57 38	57 76	35 76
19 38	39 58	77 58	77 36
39 20	59 40	59 78	37 78
21 40	41 60	19 60	Stop!
41 22	61 42	61 20	Tape,
23 42	43 62	21 62	Cut.
43 24			